How Much Should Kids Spend Online?

by Mrs. Born's class
with Tony Stead

capstone®
classroom

Kids love spending time online, but kids, teachers, parents, and experts might disagree on how much time they should spend online. Students in our class tackled the question: How much time should kids spend online? While some students think that time online should be unlimited, others believe that it should be limited unless it's for homework and research purposes. Read the opinions and think about the reasons. What do you think?

Use Your Imagination!

by Nadia

We spend so much time online, and some of this time is spent doing things that don't require our imaginations: push a button, drag and drop, type in responses. Using our imaginations is so much better than working on a computer. I'd rather listen to my imagination than a voice on a computer. Over 30 minutes a day for computer gaming is really just too long.

Think of what else you can do when you aren't on the computer. You might have a wonderful backyard or a park where you can play. Maybe you have a bike to ride or great friends to spend time with. There are many other things to do in life than sit on your pockets and look at a computer screen while you hear the clock tick away. Thirty minutes should definitely be the limit.

If you are doing something where you are gaining knowledge, not for school, but just gaining knowledge for your own good, I can understand 40 minutes on the computer. You might be planning a trip to Wichita Falls or finding information for your book report that is due on Monday or even searching for your grandmother's birthday present!

Schoolwork is a necessary component of life, and you should be able to spend time online doing research for school projects. Students of all ages, from elementary school to college, use the Internet for research. For these purposes, kids might need more time online.

Most kids my age want to spend a lot of time online, but I urge you to think carefully about this. Do you really need to spend this time online? If yes, then spend it! But if there are other ways to gain knowledge or other things to do that stretch your imagination and help you think—like getting out and enjoying life—it's best to limit your time online and live your life away from the screen!

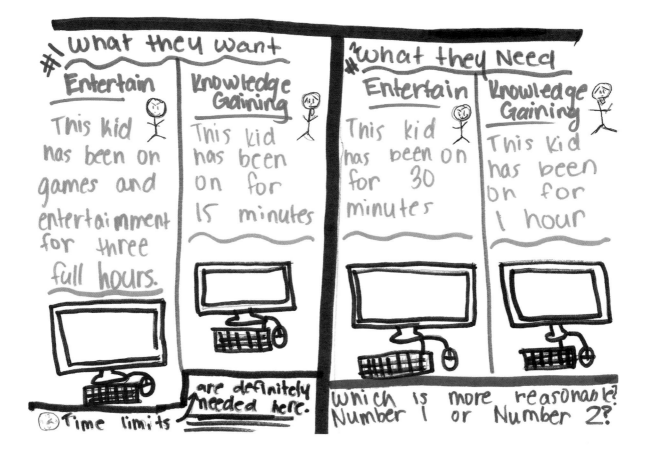

The Internet Shouldn't Rule Your Life

by Madeline

Computers have changed the world. They have also changed people's minds. With such advanced technology available all over the world, one might wonder how today's children will be affected and how much time they should spend online. In a world filled with technology, the amount of time children spend on a computer today can affect the future of tomorrow.

The Internet is a wonderful thing, but it is not something that should rule children's lives. The time that one spends on the Internet each day (which should be 1–2 hours, in my opinion) should be limited by what needs to be accomplished with this useful tool. For example, children should not use social media for an extended amount of time. Using social media can cause people to feel lonelier than they would feel without using it. Continually talking with others online makes people feel like they have been abandoned when they are away from a computer.

Children can be exposed to some awful things on the Internet if given enough time to find them. This is why time should be limited. If computer time is limited, it will be harder for children to find inappropriate things because they will be preoccupied. This also brings in the matter of social media. On social media, children may experience anonymous cyberbullying, which can affect their self-esteem.

In school, the Internet is very helpful. It makes so many things easier and more efficient. The Internet has made learning simpler with online tools and many websites about teaching. Still, students should not have to be taught entirely by machines. In addition, if students spend too long using the Internet for schoolwork, they may become bored and get off task.

Computers are not the foundation of life. They are good devices, but if children use them too much, they can be exposed to horrible things. Nobody should let his or her life be dominated by machines. That's why it is important to limit time spent online.

Be Careful on the Internet!

by Ryan

It's a place where you can find games to play, chat with your friends, read, and do research. Where is this place? The Internet! But it's a place where you need to be careful because you can spend too much time there and maybe even harm yourself.

In my opinion, you should spend no more than an hour a day online for personal stuff like games, social media, and random surfing. More than that could affect your brain, and it could keep you from doing other things that might be more valuable.

What about using the Internet for schoolwork or research? In that case, you can spend more time online. In fact, if you are really doing work, the time should be unlimited. My mom is a teacher, and she backs me up on this. If she had a time limit, she'd never get her work done!

What if you are with your friends? If time online is spent doing things together, that seems pretty valuable. You could watch a video together or find new music you both like. But wouldn't it be even more fun to play outside? Maybe you need to study together or do some chores. Think about your time online and be careful. You don't want to get carried away with it.

While the Internet is extremely useful, it's also a place where you can waste a lot of time and perhaps even be in danger from predators or thieves. Limit your time online, and use the Internet for research and studying. If you can have fun with people "live," think about doing that instead.

Kids' Ages and Time Online

by Renee

We've been thinking about time online. How much time should kids spend online? It depends on a lot of things, but their age is important. The younger the child, the less time the child should spend online. I believe it's important to limit kids' time online, especially when they are little.

Some people let their babies play games online! A very young child should be on the computer for about 10 minutes at the most. When you think about it, most babies can't sit still longer than that anyway! Kids in preschool need to do lots of things—run, play, draw. They shouldn't be online or playing games on the computer for more than a half hour a day.

When kids get to be school age, then it's important to think about their online time—time for fun and time for work. Maybe fun time should be no more than an hour a day, but then there are good reasons for kids to be online for longer. Students in elementary school might have research to do. By the time kids are in junior high and high school, they could even be running a business online. They should have more time online, because running a business is a valuable thing that could help them later on in life.

If kids are doing well with time online during the week, then it makes sense that they could get a little more time online on the weekends.

I think that kids should have limited time to spend online, but it depends on how old they are and what they are doing on the computer. The older they are and the more important the work they are doing, the more time they should be allowed to spend online.

The Internet and Your Health

by Mia

Is technology taking over children's lives? If you think about it, instead of playing outside, children seem to be spending more and more time online. The Internet is good for schoolwork, social media, and research, but I believe that limiting time online makes kids healthier.

One health risk of spending too much time online is not getting enough exercise. Instead of riding a bike, walking, taking a dance class, or playing a game outside, kids online are sitting still, moving only their fingers as they type on a keyboard or click on a mouse. The health benefits of online time are slim to none. Consequently, we have an entire generation of kids at risk for diabetes and heart disease because they spend too much time sitting still.

Spending too much time looking at a computer screen is risky for kids' eyes and brains. Eyestrain can cause headaches and the need for glasses. Brains are not as active and engaged while online. Breaks can help, but sometimes it's too late—the damage has been done.

Another problem with technology is that social media can put kids in touch with people who are risky to know. Parents worry about danger from strangers and predators, but it's even riskier sometimes to be on social media with a bully. The mean student in class could do a lot more damage than a stranger. That's a great reason to be careful about spending too much time online.

Before the Internet, people couldn't spend hours of unlimited time online, and they were still able to research, meet up with friends, read, and do all the things kids say they need time to do. I strongly believe that limiting time online is good for kids' mental and physical health.

How Much Time Should Children Spend Online?

Different Ways to Use the Internet

by Jenny

As a kid, you love being online. But health experts know it's bad for you. There are many different opinions about how long you should spend online, but it's clear that spending time online without limits is a problem. What limits make the most sense? It depends on the purpose.

If your purpose is specifically research and homework, you should spend the amount of time you need online to get the work done. Just be careful not to wander off and play games or check out social media. Stick to your purpose and make good use of your time. If you do this, your parents will be less likely to set limits. Earn their trust, and you can eventually spend more time online.

If you are using the Internet for entertainment or to catch up with people on social media, I believe that 30 minutes is enough time online. More time than that leads to eyestrain, dependence on the computer, and missing out on other things that are important and fun.

You might spend a lot of time online, but if you take action and are responsible by choosing to rest, it will help a lot. Think carefully about how you use the Internet, and the amount of time you need on it will make sense!

Kids Online

by Patrick

How long do you think kids should play online? Kids are usually on the Internet for various reasons including entertainment, schoolwork, and social stuff. In my opinion, all these things need different time limits.

When kids are on the computer just for entertainment, they should get an average of an hour. Having this much time allows us kids to play a game fully. If we only had a few minutes to play, then we would bug our parents for new games because we would never get past the first level and we'd be stuck over and over again. The same goes for gaming systems. Today's sophisticated games require more time.

If you are on the computer at home or school for school reasons, you can spend a certain amount of time online. If you are doing something that you have to finish and are working hard on, then you should be on for as long as needed. If it's not required work but still research and learning, it's OK to be on for longer than 30 minutes or so. Educational purposes are more important than gaming, and you should have more time if your online usage is for education.

Social

Schoolwork

entertainment

23

If you are using social media, a good amount of time would be 45 minutes or so. E-mail helps you keep up with your faraway family. Social media sites are places to connect with friends, join groups with causes you care about, and learn more about the world. Social media has a bad reputation, but it's not all bad! I know people who have found a pet on social media, who have met people who are their best friends now, and who have gotten help for their problems. Even my parents use it. They share photographs on social media for relatives who live far away.

How long can you be on the Internet? Education, social reasons, and entertainment are the various reasons kids are usually online. Parents and teachers can set clear and reasonable limits, and kids can always ask for more time if they have good reasons. But time limits make sense for gaming and social media use. It's important to use the Internet as wisely as you would any other resource.

Find Some Balance!

By Robert

When you are online, are you there because you want to be there? Or are you there because you need to be there? Some people believe that kids are getting addicted to spending time online. Can you have fun away from the computer? Then you probably aren't addicted to spending time online. But you should think about how much time you spend online so that you have a balanced life off and on the computer.

Sure, spending time on the computer is fun. I love being on the computer to message my friends and play games. I share photographs on social media. But when it's time to step away from the computer, I can turn it off. One of the problems with spending too much time online could be that you can't turn it off. Some kids can get crabby and unhappy if they have to get off-line. And that's really a problem.

My teacher shared her opinion with us. She told us that as much as we don't like it, kids our age need rules about using the computer. Without rules, we might not turn the computers off. And to be able to have real lives in school and with friends and in our jobs in the future, we have to be able to be away from the computer. When you apply for a job, you need to look a person in the eye, shake his or her hand, and be able to talk. If you spend too much time on the computer, you might not be able to do that!

So what's the answer to being sure kids don't spend too much time online? Kids should do their homework and chores before they go online. If you are a parent or in charge of a kid who's online, check in every 15 minutes or so to see what's going on. If a kid is online doing research or listening to good music or doing things that are appropriate, then he or she should be able to spend more time online. If not, it's time to turn off the computer.

I urge parents and kids and teachers to be sensible with time online, to help create a balance between things online and things away from the computer, and to be sure there is enough time for both. If kids get crabby away from the computer, then they may need to be given less time online, not more!

Problems with Technology

by Lisette

Is technology ruining this generation? I think it might be! Parents are talking on their phones while they drive, which causes accidents. Kids use computers to cheat or copy papers. Teens spend a lot of time on social media rather than being really social with people. How can we solve these problems? We can think very carefully about the amount of time kids spend with technology, especially how much time they spend online.

If people work efficiently, an hour or even less should be enough time for schoolwork. The same is true for games. An hour is plenty of time to spend on games online. After an hour, your eyes might hurt and your head might hurt. Besides, it's good to spend time outdoors in the sun or indoors helping your family or with your friends. When is the last time you actually sat and talked with a family member? It's important to spend time with people, not with machines. Spending time with your cat or dog is more fun than computer games after a while, and your pets need you! That's why I firmly believe that technology use should be limited.

What Kids Are doing.

What they Should be doing.

What Do You Think?

Computers are amazing tools, and there are different reasons to spend time online—for fun, for work, to read, to research, to keep in touch, to find what you need. How much time is enough time? Thirty minutes a day? An hour? More? Or even less? Consider the arguments you've read here, and then you decide. How much time should kids spend online?